THE HOPE OF
HEAVEN

STUDY GUIDE

THE HOPE OF
HEAVEN

STUDY GUIDE

HOW THE PROMISE OF ETERNITY
CHANGES EVERYTHING

SHEILA WALSH

BakerBooks
a division of Baker Publishing Group
Grand Rapids, Michigan

© 2024 by Sheila Walsh

Published by Baker Books
a division of Baker Publishing Group
Grand Rapids, Michigan
BakerBooks.com

Printed in the United States of America

Library of Congress Cataloging-in-Publication Data
Names: Walsh, Sheila, 1956– author.
Title: The hope of heaven study guide : how the promise of eternity changes everything / Sheila Walsh.
Description: Grand Rapids, Michigan : Baker Books, a division of Baker Publishing Group, [2024] | Includes
    bibliographical references.
Identifiers: LCCN 2024004275 | ISBN 9781540902801 (paper) | ISBN 9781493447084 (ebook)
Subjects: LCSH: Heaven.
Classification: LCC BT846.3 .W45 2024 | DDC 236/.24—dc23/eng/20240323
LC record available at https://lccn.loc.gov/2024004275

Cover design by Laura Powell
Cover artwork © Gold Linings by Sadie Wilson

Study guide written by Abby Perry and edited by Sheila Walsh. Based on and with material from The Hope of Heaven by Sheila Walsh.

The author is represented by Dupree Miller and Associates, a global literary agency, www.dupreemiller.com

Baker Publishing Group publications use paper produced from sustainable forestry practices and postconsumer waste whenever possible.

24   25   26   27   28   29   30   7   6   5   4   3   2   1

CONTENTS

HOW TO USE
THIS STUDY GUIDE

Welcome to the study guide for *The Hope of Heaven: How the Promise of Eternity Changes Everything*! I am delighted that you've chosen to dive deep with me into the wonderful future God has in store for those who love him.

Each session of this guide correlates with a chapter of *The Hope of Heaven*, including the introduction and conclusion. This chart will help us all stay (quite literally!) on the same page.

The Hope of Heaven	Study Guide Session
Introduction	Session 1
Chapter 1	Session 2
Chapter 2	Session 3
Chapter 3	Session 4
Chapter 4	Session 5
Chapter 5	Session 6
Chapter 6	Session 7
Chapter 7	Session 8
Chapter 8	Session 9
Chapter 9	Session 10
Conclusion	Session 11

Session Structure

This guide contains eleven sessions, each with the following sections:

- **Theme Scripture**: Our main passage for the session.
- **Reflection**: Thoughts from Sheila to open our study.
- **Word Study**: An in-depth look at a scriptural term.
- **Bridge**: A guided transition from study to application.
- **Practical Application**: Putting what we've learned into action.
- **Prayer**: Write your own and join Sheila in praying her written prayer.

Whether you're studying on your own or in a group, my prayer for you is that you will grow in hope and joy as we discover together how the promise of eternity really does change *everything*.

THINK ABOUT THE THINGS OF HEAVEN

Accompanies the Introduction
to The Hope of Heaven

We were made for more. The yearning you and I feel at times, even on our best days, is because we were made for heaven and nothing else will do.

Sheila Walsh

Theme Scripture

Since you have been raised to new life with Christ, set your sights on the realities of heaven, where Christ sits in the place of honor at God's right hand. Think about the things of heaven, not the things of earth.

Colossians 3:1–2

Reflection

What do you think about when you think about heaven?

Maybe your mind goes to reuniting with loved ones who have passed away. Perhaps you think about seeing angels or walking a street of gold. You might imagine the absence of pain or wonder what it could possibly feel like not to suffer anymore. Most of all, you are probably looking forward to seeing Jesus and being with him forever.

Whatever comes to mind when you think about heaven, I want you to know this: I am so excited to go on this journey with you to better understand heaven together and all that God has for us there. Over the past few years, the pain in this world has made me increasingly curious about the beauty of an eternity spent with Christ. In fact, Jesus's own hunger for heaven described in Hebrews 12 is part of what prompted me to grow in my knowledge of the life that awaits us, the hope of heaven.

Keep your eyes on Jesus, who both began and finished this race we're in. Study how he did it. Because he never lost sight of where he was headed—that exhilarating finish in and with God—he could put up with anything along the way: Cross, shame, whatever. And now he's there, in the place of honor, right alongside God. (Heb. 12:2–3 MSG)

Jesus never lost sight of heaven. Despite the fact that he would endure unimaginable pain, betrayal, and sorrow, Jesus kept his eyes fixed on the "joy set before him" (Heb. 12:2 NIV). Keeping his attention on heaven changed everything about his earthly life.

The same can be true for us. One thing I love about God is that he does not command us to do anything that he will not then empower us to do. So when we read in Colossians 3:2, "Think about the things of heaven," we can endeavor to do it with confidence that the Holy Spirit will equip us to set our sights on, to think about, heaven.

Before we learn more about what this looks like, let's consider what we'll be thinking about: "the realities of heaven." *The Hope of Heaven* book and this accompanying study guide will reveal what the Bible tells us and promises heaven is like:

- A real place where we will live in homes prepared for us, forever.
- Where Jesus is.
- Our eternal home, where there is fullness of joy.
- Everything we could possibly hope for, including true peace.
- Where we will see and recognize our loved ones.
- A place without shame or pain.
- The place that fulfills our every longing.
- And a lot more.

Wow! What an amazing list already. I look forward to exploring in depth each of these wonderful truths and much more throughout this study. I don't want you to just learn *about* heaven but to fill your hearts with the practical promises the hope of heaven brings each one of us.

So let's start by looking together at the phrase *think about the things of heaven* from Colossians 3:2 to discover how we can begin to establish our intentions to grow closer to the heart of God through our study of the realities of heaven. I've found through studying and researching for this book that what we have to learn about heaven will change everything about what we focus on in our lives now and especially our hope for eternity.

Which truth about heaven do you want to *think about* this week?

Why does that truth stand out to you?

Word Study: *Think About*

In each session of this study guide, we will walk through a word study. This simply means that we'll look at a word or phrase in our session's theme Scripture that has rich meaning and context when we consider it in its original language. We'll take a look at how the word is used in other passages of Scripture and paint a word picture together.

This style of Scripture study may be familiar to you, or this could be your first time giving it a try. Either way, I am confident these guided word studies can enrich your time in the Word. For me, it enriches my biblical understanding more than almost anything else.

What is your history with Bible study, if any?

What is your initial reaction to trying out a word study?

If you have any fears, uncertainties, or enthusiasm about the work to come, write a short prayer expressing those feelings to God and asking him to guide you.

Think about the Things of Heaven

The phrase *think about* in Colossians 3:2 can be translated in several different ways. Let's take a look at a few different translations and how they capture the concept:

- "set your minds" (NIV)
- "think about" (CEB)
- "look up" (MSG)
- "set your affection" (KJV)
- "give your minds" (WNT)

Each of these English phrases is based on the Greek word *phroneō* (φρονέω). This word is found in various forms throughout the New Testament. In fact, it appears twenty-six times, ranging from the Gospels to Paul's letters.

Let's take a look at some other usages of *phroneō* in Scripture. The italicized words in the following passages represent *phroneō*.

> Those who live according to the flesh *have their minds set* on what the flesh desires; but those who live in accordance with the Spirit have their minds set on what the Spirit desires. (Rom. 8:5 NIV)

> *Be of the* same *mind* toward one another; do not be haughty *in mind*, but associate with the lowly. Do not be wise in your own estimation. (Rom. 12:16 NASB)

> So it is right that I should *feel* as I do about all of you, for you have a special place in my heart. You share with me the special favor of God, both in my imprisonment and in defending and confirming the truth of the Good News. (Phil. 1:7)

> You must *have* the same *attitude* that Christ Jesus had. (Phil. 2:5; I love this one so much!)

Look up the following references. Can you find the uses of *phroneō* in these passages? You can always check your work at BlueLetter Bible.org!

Matthew 16:23   Galatians 5:10

Romans 11:20   Philippians 2:2

1 Corinthians 13:11   Philippians 4:10

2 Corinthians 13:11

Write down the verse containing *phroneō* that stands out to you.

Based on your reading, write a one-sentence definition of *phroneō*.

What might it look like to have a *phroneō* mindset about heaven?

As our word study reveals, *phroneō* does not simply describe a passing thought or a mere mention of a topic. It runs much deeper than that, painting a picture of thinking deeply about heaven.

What is one thing you can do to think about heaven this week?

How might thinking about heaven help you navigate the suffering on earth?

Bridge

The Bible tells us that one of the best ways to "think about" God and the future he has for us is through the regular study of Scripture. In the next section, we'll work together to design individualized plans for immersing ourselves in God's Word so that we can cultivate *a devoted attention* focused on the hope of heaven.

Practical Application: Studying Scripture

In each session, I'll recommend a *spiritual discipline*—a daily practice to bring you closer to God or a virtue for us to inhabit together. The idea isn't that we end our time in this study with a new to-do list filled with things we must accomplish to please God. Instead, think of these spiritual practices that we'll explore as opportunities to focus and think on the beauty of Jesus and the hope of an eternity spent in his presence. I pray this transforms your life!

Since we just walked through our first word study, I think beginning our spiritual practices with the discipline of Scripture reading—also known as *study*—seems fitting.

What have your Scripture reading habits looked like over the course of your life?

What do you enjoy about your current relationship with Scripture reading?

What would you like to change about the way you read Scripture?

In *Celebration of Discipline*, Richard Foster writes, "The purpose of the Spiritual Disciplines is the total transformation of the person. They aim at replacing old destructive habits of thought with new life-giving habits. Nowhere is this purpose more clearly seen than in the Discipline of Study. . . . The mind is renewed by applying it to those things that will transform it."*

In other words, studying Scripture is an act of thinking and focusing on God's Word.

Foster recommends four steps for study:

1. Repetition, which ingrains habits of thought
2. Concentration, which helps us to be present
3. Comprehension, which provides understanding and insight
4. Reflection, which "defines the significance" of what we study**

Consider giving these steps a try with our Colossians passage. You might engage in *repetition* by reading Colossians 3:1–2 a few times each day. *Concentration* may look like waking up before the rest of your family for some reflective time, stepping outside for a few minutes of quiet, or turning off your phone. Seek *comprehension* by reading and thinking about the passage until you feel you could

*Richard J. Foster, *Celebration of Discipline: The Path to Spiritual Growth* (New York: HarperOne, 1998), 62.
**Foster, *Celebration of Discipline*, 64–66.

explain it wisely to a friend. Finally, take some time to *reflect* on how God's perspective is on display in these verses.

In closing, write a prayer that describes the ways you want to *think about* heavenly things and study the Scriptures meaningfully. Ask God to help you as you start this learning process.

_____

_____

_____

_____

My Prayer for You

Dear God, the heaven you have created for us is so very worthy of our attention. Help us to think about and even set our minds on the beautiful future you have in store for us. Your promises are forever and your faithfulness never ending. Amen.

SESSION 2

THE JOY OF HOME

*Accompanies Chapter One
of* The Hope of Heaven

For those of us who are in relationship with Christ, the reality of heaven as our forever home should be even more real than the things we see all around us every day.

Sheila Walsh

Theme Scripture

Don't let your hearts be troubled. Trust in God, and trust also in me. There is more than enough room in my Father's home. If this were not so, would I have told you that I am going to prepare a place for you? When everything is ready, I will come and get you, so that you will always be with me where I am.

John 14:1–3

Reflection

"Home is where the heart is."

"There's no place like home."

"Home is wherever I'm with you."

Our culture is full of phrases that attempt to describe the importance, depth, and beauty of home. Dorothy clicks the heels of her ruby-red slippers in an attempt to return to familiar surroundings in *The Wizard of Oz*. Singers croon about the meaning of home, from Lynyrd Skynyrd pining for "Sweet Home Alabama" to Simon & Garfunkel wishing they were "Homeward Bound."

In film, music, and everyday conversation, people speak of home as the place where they can sigh with relief. It represents the hope of putting our feet up after a long day, eating dinner with loved ones, and curling up on the couch with a great book or favorite movie. Home is described as the great exhale, the place of our fullest comfort and joy and even safety. It's where we belong.

But for many—perhaps even for you—this ideal version of home dwells only in the imagination. In this world, home is often the place that houses our greatest conflicts. It's the place where our relationships matter most and, too often, hurt the most. It's the place where we've seen families fall apart, bills go unpaid, dreams go unfulfilled. Jesus understands that. That's why, just before he was betrayed, he strengthened his disciples' hearts by speaking to the turmoil on earth with the promise of a home in heaven, as we read in John 14:1–3. His call is the same for us: we do not need to have troubled hearts. Why? Because there is more than enough room for us in heaven. Even now, Jesus is preparing a place for us. And he will always be there with us. That's why he reminds us to trust in God and in him.

Whether your earthly homes have been places of peace, places you avoid, or somewhere in between, the truth remains the same: your heavenly home is the fullness of everything you wish home could be in this world. It is the epicenter of joy. And whether your homes on earth have reflected that joy or you are forever struggling to mirror it, I am confident that growing in your understanding of your home in heaven will give you the strength to find joy in your temporary home on earth.

As you reflect on your homes throughout your life, what words come to mind?

What questions do you have about the idea of heaven as a home?

Do you find it easy or hard to trust in Jesus and all that he has promised?

What is one way that today you can think about trusting Jesus and all he has promised you?

Word Study: *Home*

Like we did with *phroneō*, "think about," in the last session, this week we are going to look at a word in the Bible in its original language again. In doing so, we'll peel back the layers of meaning that may have occurred to the original audience of Scripture. Let's work together to paint a word picture that enriches our understanding of the biblical message.

Our word for this session is *oikia* (οἰκία), which our John 14 passage above translates as "home." *Oikia* is found ninety-five times in the New Testament and may also be translated as "house" or "household." Let's take a look at some uses of *oikia* in Scripture.

The italicized words in the passages below represent *oikia*.

> On coming to the *house*, they saw the child with his mother Mary, and they bowed down and worshiped him. Then they opened their treasures and presented him with gifts of gold, frankincense and myrrh. (Matt. 2:11 NIV)

> Knowing their thoughts, he told them, "Every kingdom divided against itself is headed for destruction, and no city or *house* divided against itself will stand." (Matt. 12:25 CSB)

> "Yes," Jesus replied, "and I assure you that everyone who has given up *house* or brothers or sisters or mother or father or children or property, for my sake and for the Good News, will receive now in return a hundred times as many houses, brothers, sisters, mothers, children, and property—along with persecution. And in the world to come that person will have eternal life." (Mark 10:29–30)

Look up the following references. Can you find the uses of *oikia* in these passages? You can always check your work at BlueLetterBible .org!

Matthew 7:24	1 Corinthians 16:15
Mark 14:3	Philippians 4:22
Luke 8:51	2 Timothy 2:20
Acts 4:34	2 John 1:10

Write down the verse containing *oikia* that stands out to you.

While looking to Scripture itself is always the place to start when we're trying to understand God's heart for us, learning from the work others have done to understand the Bible can help us as well. *Strong's Exhaustive Concordance of the Bible*, commonly known as *Strong's Concordance*, can be a useful tool, especially when studying specific words like we are doing here. *Strong's* definition of *oikia* explains that the word can refer to a residence in the abstract, but typically it is used to refer to a literal "dwelling place" and "by implication, a family."

A family. That's what the hope of heaven is for us—a dwelling place among a family who receives and welcomes us, who brings us great joy and delight, who shares the same Father and has been saved by our beloved Savior. *Oikia* conjures a domestic image: not just the house but the people who dwell, gather, and live within it. It calls to mind the joy of shared life around the dinner table and in the everyday moments that bond home dwellers together.

Based on your reading, write a one-sentence definition of *oikia*.

What might it look like to continue growing in your understanding of your heavenly *oikia*?

Let's bring our first two word studies together: What is one practical thing you can do to "think about" your heavenly "home" this week?

How might thinking about your heavenly home help you cultivate joy in your home today?

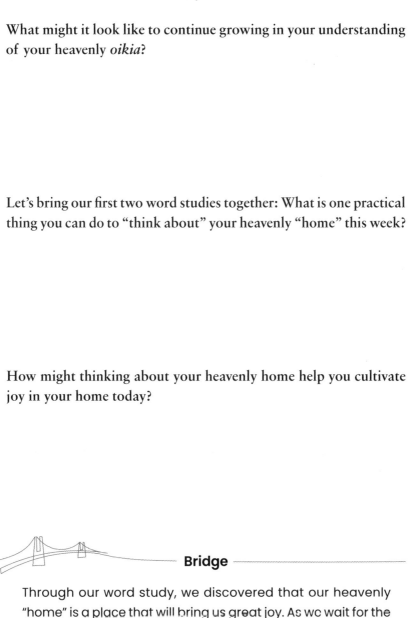

Bridge

Through our word study, we discovered that our heavenly "home" is a place that will bring us great joy. As we wait for the day when we will see Jesus face-to-face, intentionally fostering joy can help us live in light of the hope of heaven.

Practical Application: Journeying toward Joy

In light of the joy that we will experience in our forever home, this session's spiritual practice is the *cultivation of joy* in our daily lives. We can also think of this as the *practice of celebration*, which Dallas Willard describes as one of the most important, overlooked, and misunderstood disciplines of engagement.

> We engage in celebration when we enjoy ourselves, our life, our world, *in conjunction with our faith* and confidence in God's greatness, beauty, and goodness. We concentrate on *our* life and world as God's work and as God's gift to us.*

How have you practiced joyful celebration in your life and home thus far?

What challenges in your life make it hard for you to practice joyful celebration?

*Dallas Willard, *The Spirit of the Disciplines: Understanding How God Changes Lives* (New York: HarperCollins, 2000), 179.

What would you like to change about the way you practice joyful celebration?

There are many ways we might practice this joyful celebration.

1. We might start by simply praying a prayer of rejoicing or singing a joyful song during our morning commute.
2. Celebration might look like having some friends over for dinner for no real reason other than the joy of togetherness.
3. It may look like participating in a favorite activity.
4. It may also be trying something new with a friend.
5. You might find a quiet place to read Scripture out loud.
6. My favorite is singing and worshiping in the car or at church with others.

The point is not finding the perfect task to engage in joyful celebration. Instead, try asking yourself, *What brings me joy? Who brings me joy?* Then imagine the possibilities from there.

Some of us will come by joy and celebration rather naturally. Others may have to practice joyful celebration as the discipline it is until it starts to feel more ingrained. There is no bad starting point for becoming a person who practices joyful celebration. Whether your personality is to throw a party or to hide away, the joy to come in your heavenly home can serve as a spark for celebration in your life today.

What brings you joy when you are frustrated or sad?

What's something—however large or small—about understanding heaven as a home that might help you practice celebration?

How might you invite a family member or friend into the practice of celebration with you?

How can you engage more deeply in your church environment to find other ways to experience joy?

Remember that there is no start too small when it comes to cultivating a regular habit of practicing spiritual disciplines. We may be tempted to start big—throw a party! make a list of things we're thankful for every night!—but if we're not diligent, the practice can easily become a fad rather than an ongoing routine. While being open to sacrificing your time or stretching your comfort zone, consider what a sustainable practice of joyful celebration could look like in your life. Chances are, if you start with something doable, you'll grow in your practice of celebration, and those "bigger" moments will come naturally.

In closing, write a prayer describing the ways you want to let the joy of your heavenly home inspire how you live your life today. Ask God to help you practice celebration as an act of devotion to him.

_____

_____

_____

_____

My Prayer for You

God of Joy, not only do you allow us to celebrate, but you created those very experiences for our good and your glory. Help us find meaningful ways to bring about deeper joy and celebration in our lives and in the lives of others as we await the day that the joy of our eternal home will surround us every moment. Thank you that you have prepared a home for us and that you will always be there. Amen.

SESSION 3

AT PEACE IN PARADISE

*Accompanies Chapter Two
of* The Hope of Heaven

What do you believe will happen to you the moment you die? Have you ever wondered that? Do you think you simply stay in the ground until Jesus returns? Do you imagine that you might be in some disembodied limbo until the final resurrection? Scripture makes it clear that while our body stays in the ground, our spirit and soul go to be with Jesus in heaven. . . . All your loved ones who have placed their trust in Jesus are there now, with the Lord, experiencing joy and peace.

Sheila Walsh

Theme Scripture

One of the criminals hanging beside him scoffed, "So you're the Messiah, are you? Prove it by saving yourself—and us, too, while you're at it!"

But the other criminal protested, "Don't you fear God even when you have been sentenced to die? We deserve to die for our crimes, but this man hasn't done anything wrong." Then he said, "Jesus, remember me when you come into your Kingdom."

And Jesus replied, "I assure you, today you will be with me in paradise."

Luke 23:39–43

Reflection

A lot of people are afraid of death. Forty-two percent of Americans say that they fear death, and even more, 66 percent, say that the death of a loved one is their greatest fear.* It's one of the great paradoxes of being human; we know that unless Jesus happens to return in our lifetime, death will come for us all. But the inevitability of death does little to curb our fears.

In some ways, the fear of death makes sense—even for the Christian. I do not mean that we actually need to be scared of what will happen when we die. Instead, I am recognizing that death is not what we were meant to experience in the perfect world God created. Death is an intruder.

---

*Ashley Brantlet, "Demystifying Death: 7 Facts You May Not Know about Death," WellTuned, September 19, 2022, https://bcbstwelltuned.com/2022/09/19/demystifying-death-7-facts-you-may-not-know-about-death.

The Bible tells us that death entered the world through sin. Just as we were never supposed to know the gravity of evil, just as Adam and Eve were never supposed to know the shame they felt upon realizing they were naked, you and I were never meant to be acquainted with the harsh horror of death. But in Jesus we find hope that death is not our final end because sin is not our forever companion.

> For just as through the disobedience of the one man the many were made sinners, so also through the obedience of the one man the many will be made righteous. (Rom. 5:19 NIV)

While the sin of Adam drove humanity out of the garden of Eden, the righteousness of Jesus welcomes us into paradise. Though we mourn and dread the reality of death in this world, we are able to do so with the hope of those who have confidence that the life awaiting us is rich with peace. In paradise, not only will we know the absence of fear and the erasure of death, we will also know the fullness of the presence of God and the peace of everything being exactly as it should be.

What are your thoughts or feelings about death?

What comes to mind when you think about the idea of experiencing true peace in paradise?

Word Study: *Paradise*

So far in our word studies, we have learned about *phroneō*, "think about," and *oikia*, "home." Before we dive into our next biblical word, let's take some time to record our reflections on thinking about our heavenly home.

How have you fixed your mind on the thought of the home waiting for you in eternity?

What have you learned, discovered, or felt as a result of thinking about your heavenly home?

What are some of the practical ways you have "thought about" heaven since learning about *phroneō*?

What are some of the images that come to mind when you think on your heavenly *oikia*?

With *phroneō* and *oikia* fresh in our minds, let's study a word that will give us an even more complete picture of the heavenly home that invites us to think about and set our minds upon it. That word is *paradeisos* (παράδεισος), as in Jesus's words to the dying criminal on the neighboring cross: "Today you will be with me in *paradeisos*."

This is an amazing passage. Don't miss this! "Today . . . YOU . . . will be . . . WITH ME . . . IN PARADISE." Wow!

In addition to the Luke 23 passage, the New Testament includes only two other uses of *paradeisos*:

1. I know a man in Christ who fourteen years ago was caught up to the third heaven. Whether it was in the body or out of the body I do not know—God knows. And I know that this man—whether in the body or apart from the body I do not know, but God knows—was caught up to *paradise* and heard inexpressible things, things that no one is permitted to tell. (2 Cor. 12:2–4 NIV)

2. Anyone with ears to hear must listen to the Spirit and understand what he is saying to the churches. To everyone who is victorious I will give fruit from the tree of life in the *paradise* of God. (Rev. 2:7)

While the New Testament includes only these three usages of *paradeisos*, the Septuagint—the earliest surviving Greek translation of the Hebrew Bible from the original Hebrew—includes many more throughout the Old Testament.

Look up the following references. Can you find the words that the Septuagint translates as *paradeisos*? You can always check your work at BlueLetterBible.org!

Genesis 3:2	Genesis 3:23	Ezekiel 28:13
Genesis 3:3	Genesis 3:24	Ezekiel 31:9
Genesis 3:8	Nehemiah 2:8	

What images do the Septuagint passages bring to mind?

The Genesis and Ezekiel references above each contain the Hebrew word *gan* (גַּן), which is found forty-two times in the Old Testament. The word is translated as "garden." Specifically in the Genesis passages, *gan* is used for the garden of Eden. Nehemiah 2:8 sheds further light on how we might imagine paradise, as it translates the Hebrew word *pardēs* (פַּרְדֵּס) as "forest." At other times, *pardēs* is translated as "orchard."

Based on your reading, write a one-sentence definition of *paradeisos*.

What comes to mind as you think of heaven in terms of a garden?

Describe a peaceful, outdoor place where you can imagine yourself taking a big, deep breath.

Bridge

It's easy to feel like paradise is an idyllic, even mythological, place that we can't understand until eternity. But the truth is, we can taste bits of paradise as we live in light of the hope of heaven. By learning to pursue peace in our everyday lives, we can glimpse the paradise that awaits us.

Practical Application: Pursuing Peace

"Peace I leave with you; my peace I give you," Jesus tells his disciples in John 14:27 (NIV). "I do not give to you as the world gives. Do not let your hearts be troubled and do not be afraid."

Peace is such a beautiful word and one of our greatest desires. While our ultimate peace will be known only in our heavenly home, Jesus makes clear in this verse that peace is attainable even in a broken world. The word for peace often used in Scripture—*shalom*—does not merely describe the absence of conflict. Peace is not just that nothing disruptive occurs or that life carries on in a calm, smooth way. Instead, *shalom* represents the idea that everything is exactly as it should be. *Shalom* is fullness, well-being, and wholeness. It is completion and flourishing. It is, perhaps, the best way to describe what we will feel, experience, and never lose in paradise. Remember, peace is not the absence of trouble; it is the presence of Christ.

How would you describe your relationship with peace in your everyday life?

What gets in the way of your experiencing peace?

What would you like to change about your relationship with peace?

In a frenzied world, one of the ways we can begin to practice peace is through rest. For many of us, relaxation looks like crashing on the couch after a long day or finally taking the vacation we've put off for too long. But true rest—true peace—is far more than the breaks we take when we've run out of energy. Rest—like the rest God took after creation—is not simply a response to depletion. It's an intentional pause on work and activity so that we can be replenished, reflect on God's goodness, and restore our souls.

Eugene Peterson writes,

> Creation is so endlessly complex and so intricately interconnected that if we are not very careful and deeply reverent before what is clearly way beyond us, no matter how well-intentioned we are, we will probably interfere, usually in a damaging way, with what God has done and is doing. So begin by not doing anything: attend, adore.*

While peace can govern everything from our work to our hobbies, it is often the case that it begins in not doing anything but simply being present in our lives and seeking out times throughout the day to get into, experience, and attend and adore God's presence.

*Eugene Peterson, *Christ Plays in Ten Thousand Places: A Conversation in Spiritual Theology* (Grand Rapids: Eerdmans, 2008), 109.

What helps you pause, "attend," and "adore" in your life?

What might you abstain from this week in order to rest, reflect, and receive peace from God?

With the hope of full peace in paradise in mind, how might you cultivate peace in the week to come?

In closing, write a prayer describing the ways you want to let the peace of paradise draw closer to your earthly life. Ask God to help you receive and cultivate peace in your heart and relationships.

_____

_____

_____

_____

My Prayer for You

Dear God, this world is so full of trouble and distraction. Sometimes the thought of peace seems hard to grasp. May the promise of our paradise and the peace to come in eternity help us rest in this life. Thank you that, no matter what, your Son, the Prince of Peace, guaranteed our path to paradise and that we will forever be with him. Amen.

43

SESSION 4

FAITHFUL IN DISAPPOINTMENT

Accompanies Chapter Three
of The Hope of Heaven

Do you ever feel . . . frustrated, unsettled? Are you tired of it all? You got the job you'd been hoping for. You found the husband or wife of your dreams. You work so hard to provide for your family. You take that anticipated vacation. You get your children into the right college or into a job that means they can finally pay their own bills. You do it all and yet you fall into bed each night and think, *Is this all there is?* If you feel that way, I want you to know you are not alone. This is not an unnatural feeling but a deep desire for what you were actually made for.

Sheila Walsh

Theme Scripture

Sometimes we can hardly wait to move—and so we cry out in frustration. Compared to what's coming, living conditions around here seem like a stopover in an unfurnished shack, and we're tired of it! We've been given a glimpse of the real thing, our true home, our resurrection bodies! The Spirit of God whets our appetite by giving us a taste of what's ahead. He puts a little of heaven in our hearts so that we'll never settle for less.

2 Corinthians 5:2–4 MSG

Reflection

In ways both big and small, disappointment seems to be woven throughout our days. The seven-dollar latte wasn't as tasty as its price seemed to promise. The boss wasn't happy with your work, the friend who said they'd be there when you needed help was too busy, the children are struggling in school, and your spouse didn't consider your feelings when they made a decision. And then, of course, there are the ways we disappoint ourselves. We said we'd wake up early every day this week, and yet we overslept. We committed to an exercise plan then left it behind after just a few days. That to-do list we wrote with confidence and determination now finds itself buried under a pile of bills and junk mail.

Disappointment, whether with ourselves or others, is an inevitable part of our earthly lives. In fact, it's so consistent that people still quote *The Princess Bride*, one of the most beloved films of the 1980s, on the subject.

"Who are you?" a character, Inigo Montoya, asks.

"No one of consequence," another, Westley, replies.

"I must know."

"Get used to disappointment."*

Westley speaks to the inevitability of disappointment at another point in the film as he speaks to his love, Princess Buttercup. "Life is pain, highness," he tells her. "Anyone who says differently is selling something."

Here, of course, is where our Christian hope reminds us that, while disappointment in this life is inevitable, it does not dictate our whole story. God writes our stories. We cannot escape disappointment or pain this side of eternity. But, by the power of the Holy Spirit, we can put disappointment in perspective. We can lament our suffering now while trusting that the day is coming when our hurt will be no more.

Disappointment is inevitable, but it is not permanent. It began to roll away with the tombstone at the resurrection, and it will one day disappear entirely for all who put their trust in Christ. That truth can give us the perspective we need to grieve the disappointments of this life while standing on God's promises, knowing without a shadow of a doubt that he will always be faithful.

What are some of the disappointments in your life, whether big or small?

---

*The Princess Bride, directed by Rob Reiner (Los Angeles: 20th Century Fox, 1987).

How do you typically manage disappointment?

What tools have you learned that will help you handle disappointment differently? Are there certain Scriptures that you stand on during these tough times?

Word Study: *Cry Out in Frustration*

Let's take some time to review our prior word studies before we head into the next. Fill out the following chart based on your work in past sessions.

Greek word:	How you would describe the meaning of this word to a friend:	Image or concept this word evokes for you:
phroneō (φρονέω)		

Greek word:	How you would describe the meaning of this word to a friend:	Image or concept this word evokes for you:
oikia (οἰκία)		
paradeisos (παράδεισος)		

Our word studies thus far have prompted us to think about the many promises of heaven that await us. But that was just the beginning. In fact, if we string together the words we've studied into a sentence, it might sound something like, "Think about the unbelievably perfect home awaiting you in paradise." I love this! That again is the hope of heaven.

In this lesson, we're digging into the word *stenazō* (στενάζω). We see this term in 2 Corinthians 5:2–4 when Paul writes of the ways we "cry out in frustration" as we await our heavenly future. This may feel like a bit of a deviation from our earlier words, but it is so important. Take a look at the passage again. As we study this Greek word, remember that crying out is not our final destination. As Paul writes, we cry out *because* we know that what's ahead is so good. This is so encouraging to me. Like a child who has smelled the cookies baking in the oven all day but is instructed to eat their vegetables first, we quickly grow sick of the things we must do and ache for relief from obligation and disappointment. While a toddler's vegetables may not quite warrant the moaning they often get, our earthly suffering does. We are allowed to mourn, to groan, and to cry out as expressions of hope for the life to come.

Let's take a look at the various ways Bible translators have brought the term *stenazō* into English in 2 Corinthians 5:2–4:

We grow weary in our present bodies, and we long to put on our heavenly bodies like new clothing. For we will put on heavenly bodies; we will not be spirits without bodies. While we live in these earthly bodies, *we groan and sigh*, but it's not that we want to die and get rid of these bodies that clothe us. Rather, we want to put on our new bodies so that these dying bodies will be swallowed up by life.

For in this *we groan*, earnestly desiring to be clothed with our habitation which is from heaven, if indeed, having been clothed, we shall not be found naked. For we who are in this tent *groan*, being burdened, not because we want to be unclothed, but further clothed, that mortality may be swallowed up by life. (NKJV)

Here indeed *we groan*, and long to put on our heavenly dwelling, so that by putting it on we may not be found naked. For while we are still in this tent, *we sigh with anxiety*; not that we would be unclothed, but that we would be further clothed, so that what is mortal may be swallowed up by life. (RSV)

Growing weary.
Groaning.
Sighing with anxiety.

Note that Paul does not condemn the Corinthians for their expressions of disappointment. Neither does he pat them on the head and say, "It's okay." Instead, he validates their pain through the simplest yet most meaningful way we can come alongside one another in suffering: by saying "me too." Paul doesn't say, "While I have been sanctified beyond the point of disappointment, you, little children, continue to groan." No. He says, "we groan." He makes clear that the human response to having the taste of heaven lingering on our tongues is to groan until the day we experience its fullness.

How does Paul's description of *groaning* shape your desire for heaven?

Look up the following references. Can you find the usages of *stenazō* in the following passages? You can always check your work at BlueLetterBible.org!

Mark 7:34   Hebrews 13:17

Romans 8:23   James 5:9

Based on your reading, write a one-sentence definition of *stenazō*.

What might it look like for you to embrace *stenazō* as an act of faith that your future in heaven is secure?

Do you have any hesitations, concerns, or questions about the idea of practicing *stenazō*? If so, write a prayer asking God to help you. Consider bringing your thoughts to a trusted friend, pastor, or your small group for feedback.

 ── **Bridge** ────────────

Part of growing our hope for heaven is acknowledging the parts of this life that we are eager to leave behind—things like suffering, loneliness, and death. In the next section, we will take our definition of *stenazō* and discover how to put it into practice as those who look ahead to our heavenly home.

Practical Application: Learning to Long

One of the fears or concerns that Christians raise when it comes to *stenazō* is this: Isn't groaning the same thing as complaining, which we're told not to do? How can I be sure that I'm groaning for heaven without sinning? In lamenting the losses in this life, am I forgetting the promise of heaven?

While addressing these questions will look a bit different for each person, there are a few reminders that can help us all determine what it looks like to groan on this earth in light of eternity.

1. God does not ask us to do anything that he will not equip us to do. So, when his Word tells us that our hope is in heaven and yet we groan on this earth, we can trust that his character and compassion empower us to hold these truths simultaneously.

2. We can find comfort in remembering that these questions are temporary. The entire premise of groaning on earth is that we know we're made for the life to come. Groaning is not our sole form of worship, but it can be *a* form of worship as we go to God full of awareness that this life is not yet as it should be.

3. Meditating on Scripture is a great place to start learning how to long for heaven with honesty about our current disappointments and hope for our heavenly futures. The idea of meditation can feel quite loaded in our culture, as many religions and philosophies practice it in various ways. Let's demystify it a bit.

   Thomas A. Tarrants, president emeritus of the C.S. Lewis Institute, defines biblical meditation for the Christian as "a devotional practice that we engage in with God's help to know Him better, love Him more, experience closer communion with Him, and live for His glory." He explains, "In the Old Testament, two Hebrew words are translated 'meditate.' One suggests a low pitch muttering sound; the other means to be taken up or absorbed with something. Taken together, we get the idea of someone pondering a biblical text, quietly vocalizing it repeatedly."* The goal, Tarrants explains, is that the truth of God's Word might shape both our inner lives and our behavior toward others. In my own life, meditating on God's Word is where my disappointments are met by the truth of his promises.

Describe your experience with biblical meditation, if any.

If you've practiced meditation before, what was the experience like? If not, what do you imagine meditation might be like?

One of the wonderful things about meditating on God's Word is that it helps us build our reliance on the Holy Spirit. Meditation is an act of submission as, with our actions, we express to God that his Word is so rich and beautiful that it warrants our repeated attention. That ongoing focus on passages of Scripture can help us better understand the character of God. And it can help us begin to reconcile truths that sometimes feel dissonant—like the fact that we have deep disappointments and heavenly hope at the same time. Let's practice together.

*Thomas A. Tarrants, "Biblical Meditation," C.S. Lewis Institute, December 3, 2019, https://www.cslewisinstitute.org/resources/biblical-meditation.

First, take a few deep breaths and enjoy a moment of silence.

Now, read 2 Corinthians 5:2–4 at least three times.

If your setting allows, read out loud. In either case, read slowly and allow the words to settle into your heart and mind.

Did any words, phrases, or sentences stand out to you as you read? Choose one and write it here.

How might you continue to meditate on God's Word throughout your day?

I want to leave this lesson by giving you a personal example of what I do when I feel disappointed or just weary. I love to meditate on this Scripture:

> We can rejoice, too, when we run into problems and trials, for we know that they help us develop endurance. And endurance develops strength of character, and character strengthens our confident hope of salvation. And this hope will not lead to disappointment. (Rom. 5:3–5)

God's truth will not lead to disappointment.

In closing, write a prayer describing the ways you want to continue practicing biblical meditation.

My Prayer for You

Dear God, disappointments are everywhere. Surely, my brothers and sisters studying with us today are facing deep hurts and unfulfilled dreams. Help them to fix their eyes on heaven even as they have been growing weary in waiting. We trust you that relief is on its way. Amen.

SESSION 5

THE ROAD TO RELATIONSHIP

*Accompanies Chapter Four
of* The Hope of Heaven

God has invited every man, woman, and child to spend eternity with him, but it's an invitation that requires a response. He sent this invitation out in the person of his Son, Jesus Christ, a flesh-and-blood invitation with an RSVP. It's a personal invitation, it's individual. It doesn't matter where you were born or what your family believes, God has personally invited you to be in relationship with him through trusting in his Son, Jesus.

Sheila Walsh

Theme Scripture

Jesus told him, "I am the way, the truth, and the life. No one can come to the Father except through me.

John 14:6

Reflection

What keeps you from feeling like you belong?

I'm tempted to leave that question here and take us straight into our word study, but it's too important. Belonging and safety are such essential parts of the human experience that I have a hunch you could answer the question with hundreds of words of your own. As you reflect on your childhood, adolescence, young adulthood, and the years ever since, what are your stories and memories of belonging? Have you always known you were loved and safe? Have you had times of loneliness?

One of the greatest tenets of our hope for heaven is the fact that it will secure our sense of belonging throughout eternity. Notice that I said our *sense* of belonging. For those who are in Christ, the *fact* of our belonging is already secure. If you believe the gospel, you irrevocably belong to the family of God. You are never alone. You are beloved by a perfect Father. You are treasured by Christians throughout history and around the world as a brother or sister. That is all true today. And when you enter eternity, when you see Jesus face-to-face, you will never doubt it again.

You will no longer wonder if your sins are too many.
You will no longer fear that your flaws are too great.

You will no longer wish that you were someone else.

You will no longer hope to be accepted.

You will live in the fullness of joy that comes from irrevocable belonging.

In the meantime, it's likely that you will struggle to believe at all times and in all ways that your belonging is secure. When you feel yourself doubting God's love for you and your security in the family of God, turn to John 14:6, where you can be reminded of what guarantees your salvation:

> Jesus told him, "I am the way, the truth, and the life. No one can come to the Father except through me."

My salvation and certain place in heaven, this verse reminds me, do not depend on me. They depend on Jesus. And because I have trusted that he is the Way, I can come to the Father.

> I give them eternal life, and they will never perish, and no one will snatch them out of my hand. (John 10:28 ESV)

The future that awaits is secure because the way is sure.

When have you experienced a lack of belonging?

When have you experienced a strong sense of belonging?

What do you think about belonging to God?

Word Study: *The Way*

To review our word studies so far, simply freewrite a few sentences of what you recall from prior weeks. Don't worry about remembering every Greek word, exact definition, or passage. Instead, just write a reflection on the terms that come to mind. This isn't a test. It's an opportunity to notice the words that have captured your mind and heart as you cultivate the hope of heaven in your daily life.

With prior words and passages in mind, let's turn to a new word that helps us understand the certainty of our belonging in the family of God and our home in heaven. We find it in John 14:6, when Jesus calls himself "the way." In Greek, that word is *hodos* (ὁδός).

60

I am *the way*, the truth, and the life: no man cometh unto the Father, but by me. (KJV)

Take a look at the way this term is translated in other places in Scripture.

The prophet Isaiah was speaking about John when he said,

> "He is a voice shouting in the wilderness,
> 'Prepare *the way* for the LORD's coming!
> Clear the road for him!'" (Matt. 3:3)

Some people are like seed along *the path*, where the word is sown. As soon as they hear it, Satan comes and takes away the word that was sown in them. (Mark 4:15 NIV)

Look up the following references. Can you find the usages of *hodos* in the following passages? You can always check your work at BlueLetterBible.org!

Matthew 2:12	Hebrews 10:20	Jude 1:11
Mark 6:8	James 1:8	Revelation 15:3
Mark 10:46	2 Peter 2:21	

How would you describe the ways that *hodos* is used in Scripture?

In the passages above (and many more throughout the New Testament), we see that *hodos* is used to describe

- a physical road, highway, or path
- a metaphorical path
- a journey
- a manner of being or acting

Consider these in terms of John 14:6.

Jesus is the only road to the Father.

Jesus is the only way to heaven.

Jesus died so you could belong for eternity.

Our belonging is not dependent on our behavior. It is the outcome of our belief, made possible by the shed blood and resurrection of Jesus Christ. Our belief, then, is an act of acceptance. It is agreeing with God about who he says he is and about who he says we are. It is receiving the greatest gift we could ever receive. And in receiving it, we find the foretaste of eternal belonging that we will enjoy fully in eternity.

 **Bridge**

The hope of heaven is secure for those who have believed that Jesus is "the Way." For Christians, one way to keep living in accordance with that belief—not out of fear for lost salvation but out of love for God—is an ongoing habit of confessing sin and receiving forgiveness. In the next section, we will consider what it might look like to practice confession as an act of remembrance that Jesus is "the Way."

Practical Application: Confessing to Connect

The great gift of salvation is that our sins are forgiven and our severed relationship to our perfect God is restored. The practice of *confession*, telling God our shortcomings and accepting his forgiveness, is a spiritual discipline that can serve as a beautiful reminder of our belonging. Confession reminds us of the great gift we have been given and reaffirms to us—over and over and over again—that God loves us, delights in forgiving us, and has ensured our belonging with him forever.

Confession is simply the acknowledgment to God of our sin and its impact. Christian confession is not an experience that ends in shame, guilt, or self-hatred. Instead, it is an act of admitting our faults to God that we might repent of (turn from) our sins, receive God's forgiveness, and remember the love and belonging that define us.

Consider this perspective on confession and repentance from theologian, pastor, and author Timothy Keller:

In fear-based repentance, we don't learn to hate the sin for itself, and it doesn't lose its attractive power. We learn only to refrain from it for our own sake. But when we rejoice over God's sacrificial, suffering love for us—seeing what it cost him to save us from sin—we learn to hate the sin for what it is. We see what the sin cost God. What most assures us of God's unconditional love (Jesus's costly death) is what most convicts us of the evil of sin. Fear-based repentance makes us hate ourselves. Joy-based repentance makes us hate the sin.*

Notice how Keller ties the conviction of sin to our confidence in God's unconditional love. The very thing that makes our belonging secure is the thing that makes us want to turn from sin, not because we fear God rejecting us but because we are so thankful for his acceptance.

*Timothy Keller, *Counterfeit Gods: The Empty Promises of Money, Sex, and Power, and the Only Hope that Matters* (New York: Penguin Books, 2011), 172.

What stands out to you about Keller's description of repentance?

What scares you about practicing confession?

How do you practice confession?

How would you describe the relationship between confession, repentance, and belonging?

The practice of confession reminds us that our behavior is not the way to salvation. Instead *the Way* is Jesus Christ, our Friend and

Savior, whose sacrifice on our behalf serves as the path we prodigals walk on our journey to eternity with the Father. If there is anything that makes me eager to participate in joyful confession—or anything that makes me hopeful for the full sense of belonging that awaits me in heaven—it's that.

In closing, write a prayer describing the ways you want to practice confession and repentance in your daily life. Ask God to help you resist the temptation to be overcome by guilt, shame, or a sense that you do not belong in his family. Remember that Jesus is *the Way.* In him, you belong.

My Prayer for You

Dear God, in a world of rejection, sin, and difficulty, it can be so hard to remember that we belong to you. Help us to turn from the false beliefs that tell us we are not good enough to enjoy a heavenly home with you. Instead, may we be filled with the confidence that empowers joyful repentance and a deep confidence that you are eager to forgive us and welcome us into eternity with you. Amen.

SESSION 6

WORSHIP IN LIGHT OF OUR HEAVENLY HOMELAND

Accompanies Chapter Five
of The Hope of Heaven

We are buried in brokenness and raised in glory. Buried in weakness but raised in strength. Our present bodies have a limited shelf life, but our new bodies will have no expiration date. They will never let us down.

As I get older, I get frustrated that things I used to be able to do without thinking about them now need careful consideration. I have always been a huge roller-coaster fan, the bigger, the badder, the better. Now I have to think about my neck and my back surgery. Our heavenly bodies will be better than we have ever been. We'll never get tired or worn out. I don't know if there will be roller coasters in heaven or not, but if there are, I'll see you in line!

Sheila Walsh

Theme Scripture

If they had longed for the country they came from, they could have gone back. But they were looking for a better place, a heavenly homeland. That is why God is not ashamed to be called their God, for he has prepared a city for them.

Hebrews 11:15–16

Reflection

"This cookie tastes like heaven."

"The bride's bouquet was absolutely heavenly."

"A cabin deep in the woods with no cell phone service? That's what I call heaven."

People often use the term *heaven* or *heavenly* to talk about favorite things or nearly indescribable experiences. We use these words to speak of moments that feel as close to perfection as they can. We croon them over newborn babies, commenting on their heavenly little faces. In some ways, what we're saying is, this thing or person or experience is lighting up the part of our heart that knows we were made for more than what this broken world can offer.

While we use heavenly terminology in our earthly lives, we often can't quite define it in concrete terms. So we find ourselves pointing to images or concepts that might prompt us to say, "That's heavenly." There's nothing wrong with that; it's lovely to realize that we experience a little foretaste of heaven in the blessings God gives us on this earth. But we can grow even more in our heavenly hope as we look to Scripture to understand what heaven is really like. And the good news is that God has provided just what we need in his Word.

In the chapter you read this week, we covered all kinds of questions that people have about the practicalities of heaven. We considered everything from animals to angels and loved ones to little children. While there is much we will learn about heaven only when we arrive there ourselves, looking to Scripture for the answers to our questions can bring us a lot of peace and great clarity in the meantime. I hope that's what you experienced as you imagined the possibilities for what you may look like, whether your childhood dog will greet you at the pearly gates, and whether you'll be able to meet up with an angel for a walk on the streets of gold. And I hope it's what you experience when you can't find the answers you wish you could find about heaven but then remember that, no matter what else, the beautiful truth of heaven is that it is where we will see Jesus face-to-face.

Word Study: *Heavenly*

This week, we're going to look at a Greek word that will help us paint a richer picture of the heavenly life that awaits us. As we learn to meditate on God's Word, let's first review the words we've studied thus far to keep reminding ourselves of the riches we've already learned.

Fill out the following chart based on your work in past sessions.

Greek word:	How you would describe the meaning of this word to a friend:	Image or concept this word evokes for you:
phroneō (φρονέω)		
oikia (οἰκία)		
paradeisos (παράδεισος)		
stenazō (στενάζω)		
hodos (ὁδός)		

Imagine that someone asked you to describe your understanding of heaven using the word studies you've done thus far. What would you say? Don't worry about trying to copy down any Greek words. Simply use your definitions as building blocks (e.g., "I used to think of heaven as a pretty abstract, maybe even boring, place. But now I'm learning that it's a *home* in the fullest sense of the word, and that I can *think about* the *paradise* to come," etc.).

Now let's add to our list a word that you're surely going to want to weave into the description you just wrote! We find it in Hebrews 11:15–16:

> If they had longed for the country they came from, they could have gone back. But they were looking for a better place, a *heavenly* homeland. That is why God is not ashamed to be called their God, for he has prepared a city for them.

The word translated "heavenly" is *epouranios* (ἐπουράνιος). This one is helpful to break down a bit, as it comes from two words brought together: *epi* (ἐπί), which is a preposition often translated "of," and *ouranos* (οὐρανός), which is most frequently translated as "heaven" but also appears as "air" and "sky" in Scripture. Our word *epouranios*, then, roughly translates to "of heaven."

This may seem obvious at first since we know that the English *heavenly* means "of heaven" as well. But while we may know that grammatically, we likely don't give a lot of thought to what it means more deeply. In other words, what does it mean for something to be "of heaven"?

Looking at some passages that feature *epouranios* and *ouranos* can help us begin to answer that question.

Repent of your sins and turn to God, for the Kingdom of *Heaven* is near. (Matt. 3:2)

After his baptism, as Jesus came up out of the water, *the heavens* were opened and he saw the Spirit of God descending like a dove and settling on him. (Matt. 3:16)

For he raised us from the dead along with Christ and seated us with him in *the heavenly realms* because we are united with Christ Jesus. (Eph. 2:6)

Instead, they were longing for a better country—*a heavenly one.* Therefore God is not ashamed to be called their God, for he has prepared a city for them. (Heb. 11:16 NIV)

Look up the following references. Can you find the usages of *epouranios* or *ouranos* in the following passages? You can always check your work at BlueLetterBible.org!

Matthew 18:1–4   Ephesians 1:3
Luke 12:56   2 Timothy 4:18
Acts 10:12   Hebrews 11:12
1 Corinthians 15:40

How would you describe the ways that *epouranios* and *ouranos* are used in Scripture?

If you draw anything from these passages that use *epouranios* or *ouranos*, I hope it's:

1. Jesus and the New Testament writers spoke of heaven and heavenly things *regularly*, which means they're important for us to remember.
2. The things of heaven are often described as the opposite of, or at least outside of, the things on earth.
3. Heaven is a kingdom where God reigns.
4. Heaven is where we will see Jesus face-to-face.

If you're feeling eager for more passages that describe heaven, try this: Read through Revelation 21 and 22 at your normal reading speed. Next, get a piece of paper and a pen. Then read the chapters again, making a bulleted list of everything that appeals to your senses—what can you see, hear, taste, touch, smell? Once you've made your list, read through it and pick a characteristic or two that you want to keep thinking on this week. It could be something architectural, like "the city is laid out as a square"; geographic, like "the sea is no more"; or cultural, such as "the nations of those who are saved shall walk in its light." Whatever you choose to reflect on, may it multiply your anticipation of the heavenly home that awaits you.

 **Bridge**

Our study of *epouranios* and *ouranos* makes me so excited about the eternity that awaits us in heaven. I hope you're feeling the same! Whether you're eager to express your joy or in need of an activity that might help you cultivate some enthusiasm, today's application section is for you. May it help us bring what we know about heaven into worship on earth.

Practical Application: Walking in Worship

Toward the end of chapter 5 of *The Hope of Heaven*, we considered what worship will be like in heaven. We walked through the ways that John describes worship both in the book of John and in Revelation, where a few key themes emerge. Chief among them is this: the worship we will experience in eternity is pure, transparent, and without distraction. We will fix our eyes on Jesus with no desire to look elsewhere. What a glorious day that will be.

What might it look like for you to practice the spiritual discipline of wholehearted *worship* in the weeks to come? In an article entitled "Seven Everyday Ways to Worship the Lord," writers Jocelyn Seybold and Millicent Martin Poole offer some ideas:

- Admire the wonders of nature.
- Set aside a period of silence to the Lord.
- Read Scripture aloud.
- Memorize Scripture.
- Sing a song of praise.
- Love others.
- Pray through a Psalm out loud.*

Which of these ideas would you like to put into practice this week?

---

*Jocelyn Seybold and Millicent Martin Poole, "Seven Everyday Ways to Worship the Lord," Voice Dallas Theological Seminary, updated July 7, 2006, https://voice.dts.edu/article /seven-everyday-ways-to-worship-the-lord-millicent-poole-and-joycelyn-seybold/.

What might it look like for you to prioritize your practice of worship in the days to come?

Have any other ideas for worship come to mind? If so, write them—as well as a practical plan for practicing them—here.

In closing, write a prayer describing the ways you want to practice worship in your daily life. Ask God to help you worship in light of the fact that, one day, you will see his Son face-to-face.

My Prayer for You

Dear God, this world is full of distractions. But someday, all we will see are you and the heavenly home you have created for us. Help us to worship in light of that truth even now, knowing that the day when we will experience the truest worship imaginable is coming soon. Amen.

SESSION 7

LONGING FOR HEAVEN

*Accompanies Chapter Six
of* The Hope of Heaven

One of the most amazing things about being free of sin and struggles will be finally being who God created us to be. Do you ever get tired of yourself? I know I do at times. I get frustrated when I fall into the same old patterns or react in the same old way. I get tired of thinking in the same way. What about you? Whatever it is about yourself that you find frustrating or discouraging will be gone. There will be no more self-doubt or fear or sadness. You'll be the beautiful, creative, joy-filled you that God created you to be.

Sheila Walsh

Theme Scripture

How lovely is your dwelling place,
O Lord of Heaven's Armies.
I long, yes, I faint with longing
to enter the courts of the Lord.
Psalm 84:1–2

Reflection

When was the last time you waited for something with such eager anticipation that it nearly consumed your thoughts? It could have been something exciting, like an event you bought tickets for long ago that's finally drawn close. Maybe you remember awaiting your wedding day, the morning of your new job, or the birth of a child or grandchild.

There are times when waiting is such an all-consuming experience that we find ourselves able to do little else except, well, wait.

This, of course, is where the idea of becoming "so heavenly minded that we're no earthly good" comes to mind. We may fear that if we wait for heaven with too much fervor, we will stop paying attention to things that matter here on earth. At the risk of sounding glib, I don't think this is going to happen. I especially don't think it will be the case for those of us who do the sacred work you're doing now: the work of understanding what heaven will be like. Understanding heaven's complete and perfect goodness is not something that distracts us from living righteously on earth. In fact, it offers us the opposite experience: hope for the future that is so rich and comprehensive, it gives us the strength and grace we need to live godly lives.

In this session, we'll consider what it looks like to yearn for heaven. Our eternity with God is unparalleled in its magnificence. Let's learn to long for it.

Word Study: *Longing*

This week, we get to look at a pair of Hebrew and Greek words that the Bible uses to describe longing. Before we dive into these ancient languages, take some time to describe longing in your own terms.

How would you define longing?

What images come to mind when you picture longing?

What are some of your personal experiences with longing?

In Psalm 84:1–2, we find the psalmist articulating a deep, consuming desire for heaven.

> How lovely is your dwelling place,
> O Lord of Heaven's Armies.
> I long, yes, I faint with longing
> to enter the courts of the Lord.

The word the psalmist uses for "longing" is the Hebrew *kasaph* (נִכְסַף). Let's take a look at a few other translations of this passage to begin broadening our perspective of what it means to long.

> My soul *yearns*, even faints,
> for the courts of the Lord;
> my heart and my flesh cry out
> for the living God. (v. 2 NIV)

> *I desperately want* to be
> in the courts of the Lord's temple.
> My heart and my entire being shout for joy
> to the living God. (v. 2 NET)

> *The passion of my soul's desire* is for the house of the Lord; my heart and my flesh are crying out for the living God. (v. 2 BBE)

The word *kasaph* is found in a few other places in the Old Testament, including Job 14:15:

> You would call and I would answer,
> and you would *yearn* for me, your handiwork.

Then, in the New Testament, we find the word *epipotheō* (ἐπι-ποθέω) used to represent longing. In the Septuagint, the translators used *epipotheō* for *kasaph*.

I love this verse:

> We grow weary in our present bodies, and *we long* to put on our heavenly bodies like new clothing. (2 Cor. 5:2)

We are longing for heaven.

Now look up the following references. Can you find the usages of *kasaph* or *epipotheō* in the following passages? You can always check your work at BlueLetterBible.org!

Genesis 31:30	2 Corinthians 9:14	2 Timothy 1:4
Romans 1:11	Philippians 1:8	James 4:5

Based on the usages of *kasaph* or *epipotheō* that you've read, how would you define longing?

Write your own translation of Psalm 84:1–2.

Nineteenth-century Christian leaders J. J. Stewart Perowne and C. H. Spurgeon offer powerful insights into this passage. Perowne writes,

Soul . . . heart . . . flesh. Marking the whole man, with every faculty and affection. The verbs are also very expressive. The first "longeth," means literally, "hath grown pale," as with the intensity of the feeling; the second, "fainteth," is more exactly "faileth," or "is consumed."[*]

And Spurgeon writes,

When he says that his flesh cried out for the living God, he does not mean flesh in the sense in which Paul uses the term, for in that flesh there dwells no good thing, but the Psalmist means to express here the whole of his nature, "My soul, my heart, and my flesh." The combination of his entire manhood—spirit, soul and body—was moved with such intense agony of desire that it must express itself and it could only express itself in a cry, "My heart and my flesh cries out for the living God."[**]

[*]J. J. Stewart Perowne, *The Book of Psalms, Volume 2* (London: G. Bell & Sons, 1871), 115, https://www.blueletterbible.org/Comm/spurgeon_charles/tod/ps084.cfm, italics in the original.
[**]C. H. Spurgeon, "Grace and Glory," Metropolitan Tabernacle, London, May 17, 1885, https://ccel.org/ccel/spurgeon/sermons43/sermons43.v.html.

Add your own paragraph of commentary for Psalm 84:1–2. Don't worry about sounding like Perowne, Spurgeon, or anyone but yourself.

 **Bridge**

The experience of longing can feel lonely and even isolating. As we take what we've learned about longing for heaven into our application section, we find that God is eager to meet us in a deep relationship through prayer. He understands our every desire and is here to listen to our yearning hearts.

Practical Application: Persisting in Prayer

Ah, the power of prayer. What a supernatural spiritual discipline. While we often think of the phrase in terms of the ability to ask God for specific outcomes, the power of prayer is not limited to that realm. Prayer transforms *us*, especially as we pray God's will. Whether or not our circumstances change or the thing we wish for comes true, prayer does not fail, because the God who meets with us in prayer is a God of victory. His love and communion with us are miracles in themselves.

This does not mean that the things we pray for are unimportant or unworthy of bringing to God. On the contrary, because God loves us, he loves when we pour our hearts out to him about our hurts, hopes, and everything in between. Even still, as we grow in our practice of prayer, we are given the opportunity to discover that prayer's power to deepen our relationship with God and our confidence in him is the thing that keeps us turning to him. It is the thing that urges us to yearn for God and to long for heaven.

What is your prayer life like?

How has your relationship with prayer changed over time?

Do you enjoy prayer? Be honest! It's normal to find prayer boring, confusing, or forgettable. The great news is that it doesn't have to stay that way.

In *The Divine Conspiracy*, theologian Dallas Willard wrote a passage on prayer that is as simple as it is stunning:

> I believe the most adequate description of prayer is simply, "Talking to God about what we are doing together." That immediately focuses

the activity where we are but at the same time drives the egotism out of it. Requests will naturally be made in the course of this conversational walk. Prayer is a matter of explicitly sharing with God my concerns about what he too is concerned about in my life. And of course he is concerned about my concerns and, in particular, that my concerns should coincide with his. This is our walk together. Out of it I pray.*

Reread the Willard passage a few times. On your third or fourth read-through, underline the phrases that stand out to you, then write them below.

How does Willard's description differ from or comport with your understanding of prayer?

I think my favorite thing about Willard's description of prayer is the phrase "this is our walk together." This is the part of his explanation that gets me thinking about heaven because it is so beautiful to imagine that our walk with God in prayer starts here and continues on in a seamless manner when we enter eternity. Today, we walk with God through prayer. We express our longing for heaven.

*Dallas Willard, *The Divine Conspiracy: Rediscovering Our Hidden Life in God* (New York: HarperCollins, 1998), 243.

In eternity, we will walk with God in fullness of experience, conversation, and connection. There will be no fear that we are doing it wrong. There will be no guilt or shame over what we share or confess. There will simply be an ongoing walk that hearkens back to the fellowship Adam and Eve experienced with God in the garden of Eden before the fall.

How might thinking about prayer in light of heaven change the way you pray?

How would you like to practice prayer this week?

In closing, write a prayer describing the ways you want to practice prayer in your daily life. Ask God to help you pray as one who is on a walk with him.

My Prayer for You

Dear God, "this is our walk together." That is the way I hope that all who love you will live, trusting that you are delighted by our fellowship and eager to share your love and attention with us. Help us to remember that we are headed for a future you designed for us that is defined by your love for us. Amen.

SESSION 8

SERVING IN LIGHT OF ETERNAL REWARDS

Accompanies Chapter Seven of The Hope of Heaven

Did you know that every believer will stand before the judgment seat of Christ, not to be punished but to be rewarded? This is so important to me. I want you to understand that this will happen. Your life matters. Everything you do for Christ, whether anyone on earth notices or not, God does. I have met hundreds of people through the years who are quietly serving God, showing up in ways that are seldom recognized, but I know that their day is coming when Christ himself will reward them. I want that to be you!

Sheila Walsh

Theme Scripture

Look, I am coming soon, bringing my reward with me to repay all people according to their deeds. I am the Alpha and the Omega, the First and the Last, the Beginning and the End.

Revelation 22:12–13

Reflection

Have you ever worked hard for something that never came? Perhaps you spent years doing everything you could to earn a promotion, then it was given to someone else. Maybe you gave your best to a romantic relationship only to have the person leave. It could be that you devoted yourself to being a great parent and then your child wandered away from the faith. You may have dedicated countless Sundays to volunteering in your church only to have someone else receive the leadership position.

As painful as these experiences are, it's often an added layer that makes them excruciating: feeling as though the loss was unseen. Sure, it stung not to get the promotion, but what felt even worse was the sense that your boss didn't notice how hard you had been working. Of course the breakup hurt, but the feeling that you lost years of your life to a future that would never come was the thing that made it hard to get out of bed in the morning.

Feeling unseen when we have tried our best is a deeply painful experience. It's also one that we will never experience in heaven.

When we think about the fact that God is watching us, most of those thoughts are comforting. But some of us are quick to think about the way he sees our sins or struggles or the fact that he can read the thoughts we would never speak aloud. This view of God, though, keeps us from seeing the incredible truth that he sees every last faithful thing we do. He sees our diligence at work and our devotion at home. He sees our investment in relationships with friends who can't always give back to us in the ways we give to them. He sees our decades of dedication to our churches. He sees it all. And one day, he will bestow eternal rewards on us that cannot be taken away. Remember, he is a good, good Father.

Word Study: *Reward*

Let's review the words we've studied thus far.

Fill out the following chart based on your work in past sessions.

Hebrew or Greek word:	How you would describe the meaning of this word to a friend:	Image or concept this word evokes for you:
phroneō (φρονέω)		
oikia (οἰκία)		
paradeisos (παράδεισος)		

Hebrew or Greek word:	How you would describe the meaning of this word to a friend:	Image or concept this word evokes for you:
stenazō (στενάζω)		
hodos (ὁδός)		
epouranios (ἐπουράνιος)		
kasaph (כָּסַף) *epipotheō* (ἐπιποθέω)		

Choose one or two of the terms above. Write a few sentences about the way these biblical terms have helped you grow in your hope for heaven.

Today's Greek word is found in the final chapter of the Bible—
Revelation 22. While many look to the book of Revelation for insight
into the end times (and there are good reasons to do so!), for our
purposes here I want us to keep our minds focused on what this passage has to say about something that many Christians aren't aware
of—the rewards that await us in heaven.

> Look, I am coming soon, bringing my *reward* with me to repay all
> people according to their deeds. I am the Alpha and the Omega, the
> First and the Last, the Beginning and the End.

The focus of today's word study is *misthos* (μισθός), translated here
as "reward." Let's take a look at a few more passages in the New
Testament that use *misthos*:

> Rejoice and be glad, because great is your *reward* in heaven, for in
> the same way they persecuted the prophets who were before you.
> (Matt. 5:12 NIV)

> When evening came, the owner of the vineyard told his foreman,
> "Call the workers and give them their *pay*, starting with the last and
> ending with the first." (Matt. 20:8 CSB)

> Even now the one who reaps draws a *wage* and harvests a crop for
> eternal life, so that the sower and the reaper may be glad together.
> (John 4:36 NIV)

**Look up the following references. Can you find the usages of *mist-
hos* in the following passages? You can always check your work at
BlueLetterBible.org!**

Acts 1:18   1 Corinthians 3:8

Romans 4:4   1 Timothy 5:18

James 5:4   Revelation 11:18

Jude 1:11

What did you notice about uses of *misthos* in the Bible?

One thing that stands out to me is the way that *misthos* does not simply refer to rewards for doing something right. It is used to describe the proper payment or wage for an action or a job. Here is a helpful example of something we should keep in mind as we conduct word studies: It's easy for us to apply moral meaning to every word we read in the Bible because, well, it's the Bible! But one of the beautiful things about Scripture is that, while it is entirely inspired by God, it uses human terms designed for humans to understand.

In this case, when we read *misthos*, we can think of wages or payment. We know what it feels like when a job has been done well and is rightly compensated. We know what it feels like when someone does a poor job—or even an evil job—and yet still receives payment for it. The beautiful thing about heaven is that there (and only there), *misthos* will refer to rewards for righteousness. There will no longer be anyone trying to receive payment they did not earn, nor will there be hard workers who continually go underpaid or unseen. There will be fullness of truth and a God who takes great joy in rewarding his children for their jobs well done.

 **Bridge**

This session's theme Scripture explains that our earthly righteousness can lead to rewards in heaven. As a reminder, the reward is not a place in heaven—that is secured by the shed blood and resurrection of Jesus Christ. Therefore, we can serve others from a place of joyful confidence, eager to help and willing to sacrifice, because our reward in heaven is great.

Practical Application: Serving Faithfully

Are you feeling nervous? If so, it's okay. The thought of *service* as a spiritual discipline can make a lot of us squirm a bit as we wonder if we're doing enough, doing it right, or need to be doing something different. As we begin to consider how we might cultivate service as a spiritual practice in our lives, take care to remember that the goal of your service is not to achieve an earthly standard of success. Instead, it is simply to be faithful to the opportunities God places before you with the knowledge that, in doing so, your reward in heaven awaits.

How are you serving in your church, family, community, or elsewhere?

What do you enjoy about serving? This could be anything from certain tasks to the opportunity to build relationships. Many times, we find it hard to start. Ask God to open doors of service for you.

Our Western culture has a high view of philanthropy, but that often does not carry over into an appreciation for humble service. While beautiful charity galas and large-scale nonprofit efforts can be wonderful things, most of us will find ourselves more regularly serving in quiet ways that feel small. This is where remembering heaven matters so much because when the moment comes for us to receive rewards from our heavenly Father, there will be no such thing as a small act of faithfulness. There will only be the proud smile of a loving God who is delighted that we obeyed his calling on our lives.

Richard Foster notes that service can be hard to capture in words and is instead one of those "you know it when you see it" types of things. He writes,

> When we see someone intently listening to another human being, we are witnessing service in action. When we see a person holding the sorrows of another in tender, loving care, we are witnessing service in action. When we see someone actively guarding the reputation of others, we are witnessing service in action. When we see simple, everyday acts of kindness, we are witnessing service in action. It is in these actions and many more like them that we begin to get a picture of service.*

*Richard J. Foster, from the foreword to Nathan Foster, *The Making of an Ordinary Saint: My Journey from Frustration to Joy with the Spiritual Disciplines* (Grand Rapids: Baker Books, 2014), 119.

Underline any of Foster's examples that stood out to you. What feels important or meaningful to you about those examples?

How might you cultivate service as a spiritual practice in your life this week?

How might engaging in service foster your hope for heaven?

In closing, write a prayer describing the ways you want to practice service in your daily life. Ask God to help you serve as one who knows your reward is in heaven.

_____

_____

_____

_____

My Prayer for You

Dear God, it can feel so hard when our efforts seem to go unseen. Help us to remember that you see it all and that our reward for faithfulness is coming—not randomly, or if you happen to remember, but as your direct acknowledgment of and delight in our obedience. You are a faithful God. Amen.

SESSION 9

UNENDING SIGHT IN THE NEW HEAVEN AND NEW EARTH

Accompanies Chapter Eight of The Hope of Heaven

We will rest. What a beautiful thought. Our days will be filled with the most fulfilling work we've ever known and then the joy of rest. I imagine picnics by a river in fields of the greenest grass I've ever seen. I think of watching animals playing together, tumbling over one another, and then resting in a heap. I think of popping in to see friends, lavish meals around an open fire, and conversations like we've never known before. This is not wishful thinking. This is our solid hope, and so we keep walking. We keep taking the next step even as we long for a glimpse of the shore.

Sheila Walsh

Theme Scripture

I saw no temple in the city, for the Lord God Almighty and the Lamb are its temple. And the city has no need of sun or moon, for the glory of God illuminates the city, and the Lamb is its light. The nations will walk in its light, and the kings of the world will enter the city in all their glory. Its gates will never be closed at the end of day because there is no night there. And all the nations will bring their glory and honor into the city. Nothing evil will be allowed to enter, nor anyone who practices shameful idolatry and dishonesty—but only those whose names are written in the Lamb's Book of Life.

Revelation 21:22–27

Reflection

Have you ever had a day of travel that seemed as though it would not end? Maybe your flight home from a business trip was delayed. Perhaps you were road-tripping with your family and the highways were jammed with stop-and-go traffic. All you could think about was that moment when you would pull into the driveway, walk into the house, and embrace the comforts of being home. Maybe you pictured your favorite chair and a bowl of popcorn. Maybe you imagined taking a long, hot shower before crawling into your own bed with your own pillow. *Just get me home.*

When travel feels like it will never end, our awareness of the specific delights of home sharpens immensely. The same can be said for our journey toward heaven. As we grow tired of hard work, challenging relationships, and circumstances we would never choose, we may find ourselves more eagerly yearning for the rest that awaits us in eternity. Like the weary dad who has been driving his family across the country or the exhausted businesswoman just trying to get home in a snowstorm, we find ourselves whispering, *Just get me home.*

Our desire for home is not merely a craving for difficulties to cease. When we return from travel, we aren't content to sit in our cars outside the house. It's not fulfilling enough that the hard part is over. No, we were made for more. We want the security and joy and comfort of being *home*. The beauty of heaven is not only the ceasing of earthly strife but also the fulfillment of our greatest hopes to belong, to be safe, and to be loved. And as we grow in delighting in what awaits us in heaven, we find greater endurance for the journey toward it.

Word Study: *Illuminates*

We've studied a lot of words together thus far! To keep them top of mind as we add another to our list, take some time to write about the biblical terms you've learned so far. Don't worry about remembering every Greek word, exact definition, or passage. Instead, just write a reflection on the terms that come to mind. Remember, like I said in session 5, this isn't a test. It's simply an opportunity to notice the words that have captured your mind and heart as you cultivate the hope of heaven in your daily life.

Our next term is one that appears in Revelation 21:22–27. The Greek word is *phōtizō* (φωτίζω), which comes from the root word *phōs* (φῶς), often translated "light." While *phōs* is a noun, *phōtizō* is a verb. As we study this further, you will see not only that God is illuminating our hearts now but also that we will live in heaven with God's light forever. Fear is forever gone. Darkness is gone. Until then, he will light our path.

What might be some other verb forms of *light*?

If you guessed something like *illuminate* or *enlighten*, you're right on. Let's take a look at some additional uses of *phōtizō* in Scripture to further illuminate (ha!) our understanding of the term.

Therefore, if your whole body is full of light, and no part of it dark, it will be just as full of light as when a lamp *shines its light* on you. (Luke 11:36 NIV)

This was the true Light that, coming into the world, *enlightens* every person. (John 1:9 NASB)

I pray that your hearts will be *flooded with light* so that you can understand the confident hope he has given to those he called—his holy people who are his rich and glorious inheritance. (Eph. 1:18)

And *to make all see* what is the fellowship of the mystery, which from the beginning of the ages has been hidden in God who created all things through Jesus Christ. (Eph. 3:9 NKJV)

Look up the following references. Can you find the usages of *phōtizō* in the following passages? You can always check your work at BlueLetterBible.org!

1 Corinthians 4:5	Hebrews 6:4	Revelation 18:1
2 Timothy 1:10	Hebrews 10:32	Revelation 22:5

How would you describe the ways that *phōtizō* is used in Scripture?

The Revised English Bible and Commentary notes that, in his book *Word Pictures*, A. T. Robertson describes *phōtizō* as a later Greek verb that means "to turn the light on."

Thus it was used as "to bring to light," "to give light," "to light up," "to inform, teach, give understanding to." The Sacred Secret was hidden in God until God told Paul and he in turn instructed others about it, so "to bring to light and teach about" would be a good understanding of the fuller meaning of the verb in this context.*

Just as we turn on a light to help us see and learn what surrounds us, so God will illuminate the entire kingdom of heaven in eternity. Nothing will be shadowed or shrouded any longer, so we will not fear what lurks in shadows. The God who now illuminates our hearts with the truth of the gospel will illuminate our very sight as we spend eternity with him.

*The Revised English Version, accessed November 5, 2023, https://www.revisedenglish version.com/Ephesians/chapter3/9#.

 **Bridge** ————————————

One of the incredible implications of God as our light in heaven is this: We will no longer have secrets from one another. Everything will be made plain and, even better, we'll *want* it to be that way. We won't fear sharing parts of ourselves. We will live fully and freely in the light, illuminated by God himself, and we will participate in joyful connection with our brothers and sisters as they, too, dance in the light. In our application section, we'll consider what it looks like to live in the light with our Christian community on earth.

Practical Application: Fostering Fellowship

As we await the day when we will never again fear judgment or exclusion or wonder if our belonging is hanging in the balance, fostering fellowship with one another as a spiritual practice can more deeply root our hope for heaven. Spending time with fellow believers is important for a host of reasons, including walking as the Scriptures encourage us to walk. The writer of Hebrews guides Christians to meet together so that we can encourage one another (10:25). Jesus modeled intentional community as he surrounded himself with the twelve disciples, regularly ate meals with others, and conducted a great deal of his ministry in a relational context. The early church broke bread together, shared their resources, and grew in wisdom through teaching and praying together.

Of course, fellowship can be complicated. Being vulnerable with other people opens us up to conflict and pain. But it also gives us the opportunity to practice the beautiful community we will experience in eternity when all of the insecurities, sin, and disagreements that harm relationships are no more.

What have your experiences of Christian fellowship been like?

What would you like to see change about your habits of fellowship?

When you think about enjoying fellowship, who comes to mind? What are you doing together?

How might you pursue deeper Christian fellowship in the coming days or weeks?

A word of encouragement for those of us who struggle with fellowship: fellowship isn't *hosting*. It isn't about creating a perfect environment designed to impress our guests. Instead, fellowship is about joint participation in meaningful relationships, which can happen anywhere. While some of us will love welcoming people into our homes regularly, others will find themselves better able to relax and connect in a coffee shop, on a fishing trip, or while taking a walk around the neighborhood. Fellowship can look like serving together, relaxing together, and even being quiet together. The medium of fellowship isn't what matters most. The message—that we belong to Christ and to each other—that's what matters.

In closing, write a prayer describing the ways you want to practice fellowship in your daily life. Ask God to help you cultivate community as one who looks forward to perfect relationships in heaven.

My Prayer for You

Dear God, we long for the day when your perfect light illuminates our path. Until then, help us to look to the Scriptures, prayer, and fellowship as the blessings they are. Help us to find the glimpses of light you offer us now, trusting that one day all will be bright. Amen.

SESSION 10

HIDDEN FOR HEAVEN

Accompanies Chapter Nine
of The Hope of Heaven

To be with Jesus, to see him as he is, all the time, is beyond my ability to fathom. If you're like me, there are days when you feel God's presence so close, but there are also days when he seems so far away. There are days when it's easy to believe that God is good and merciful and loving, but I know there can be days when that's harder. When you've prayed and prayed for the healing of a loved one or you're doing all you can to provide for your family, but it feels as if your prayers are not being heard, it's easy to struggle with what you don't understand. Those days are coming to an end. When we see Jesus face-to-face, when God himself comes down to earth to live with us, to be with us, we will never have a moment of doubt or pain again.

Sheila Walsh

Theme Scripture

For you died to this life, and your real life is hidden with Christ in God. And when Christ, who is your life, is revealed to the whole world, you will share in all his glory.

Colossians 3:3–4

Reflection

If there's one children's game that has stood the test of time, it has to be hide-and-seek. Children seem to find something infinitely, essentially delightful about scurrying off to tuck themselves away as they wait for their friends to find them. The squeals of delight upon being found are unparalleled. The excitement of being hidden is outmatched only by the glee of being revealed.

In many ways, so it is in our relationship with Christ. We are hidden with him in God, as Colossians 3 says, and it is there that we are safe, held, and loved. The blessing of that security will only be outdone on the day when the Christ who hides with us is revealed to the whole world and takes his rightful place as King over all. As he does, we, too, will be revealed in glory, losing none of our safety, belonging, or love but getting to experience them in utter fullness.

Can you imagine? What a day that will be!

Word Study: *Hidden*

This is the last time we'll review our words together, as I want us to focus solely on one term in our final session. So let's soak up this opportunity to recap what we've learned about terms in Scripture!

Fill out the following chart based on your work in past sessions.

Hebrew or Greek word:	How you would describe the meaning of this word to a friend:	Image or concept this word evokes for you:
phroneō (φρονέω)		
oikia (οἰκία)		
paradeisos (παράδεισος)		
stenazō (στενάζω)		
hodos (ὁδός)		
epouranios (ἐπουράνιος)		

Hebrew or Greek word:	How you would describe the meaning of this word to a friend:	Image or concept this word evokes for you:
kasaph (כָּסַף) epipotheō (ἐπιποθέω)		
misthos (μισθός)		
phōtizō (φωτίζω)		

Choose as many or as few of the terms above to weave together into a paragraph or two. Write about how these words help you look forward to heaven.

Finally, take some time to reflect on the act of conducting word studies. What has it taught you? How might you continue to study words in the Bible going forward?

Now that we've reviewed our list of words thus far, let's dive into a dynamic word found in Colossians 3:3–4.

For you died to this life, and your real life is *hidden* with Christ in God. And when Christ, who is your life, is revealed to the whole world, you will share in all his glory.

The word translated "hidden" is *kryptō* (κρύπτω). Sound familiar? There are a lot of English words that draw on this Greek word, including *cryptographer* and *cryptocurrency*.

Based on your knowledge of English *krypto/crypto* words, what terms or images come to mind about *kryptō*?

Let's take a look at a few more usages of *kryptō* in the Bible:

You are the light of the world—like a city on a hilltop that cannot be *hidden*. (Matt. 5:14)

The kingdom of heaven is like treasure, *buried* in a field, that a man found and reburied. Then in his joy he goes and sells everything he has and buys that field. (Matt. 13:44 CSB)

Later, Joseph of Arimathea asked Pilate for the body of Jesus. Now Joseph was a disciple of Jesus, but *secretly* because he feared the Jewish leaders. With Pilate's permission, he came and took the body away. (John 19:38 NIV)

Look up the following references. Can you find the usages of *kryptō* in the following passages? You can always check your work at BlueLetterBible.org!

Matthew 13:35	John 8:59	Revelation 2:17
Matthew 25:25	1 Timothy 5:25	Revelation 6:15
Luke 19:42	Hebrews 11:23	

What are some of the ways that *kryptō* is used in Scripture?

One of the things that *kryptō* can teach us about studying biblical words is how often a word that is literal and physical can also be metaphorical. In Hebrews 11:23, for example, we see the word *kryptō* used to describe how Moses's parents literally and physically hid him for three months as an infant. Passages in John describe Jesus literally being hidden from crowds. But then, in Luke 18, for example, we see *kryptō* used to describe words being hidden from people as they fail to understand their meaning.

> The disciples did not understand any of this. Its meaning was hidden from them, and they did not know what he was talking about. (v. 34 NIV)

This array of usages of *kryptō* leads me to think about passages in the Old Testament where "hiddenness" seems to be a theme—again, sometimes literally and sometimes metaphorically. I think about the prophets, whose messages were partially understood but had fuller meaning that was hidden from their hearers. I think about David hiding in a cave (1 Sam. 22). I think about God speaking to Moses in Exodus, telling Moses that he will hide him "in a cleft in the rock" when his glory passes by (33:21–23 NIV).

These rich images grow my affection for the fact that, as a believer in Jesus, I am hidden with Christ in God. They enhance my understanding of how protected I am, of how safe and secure my place in heaven is. I hope they do the same for you.

What does it mean to you to be hidden in Christ?

 **Bridge**

As those who are hidden in Christ, we are released from the need to strive our way into the spotlight. The protection that God provides us by ensuring our place in heaven gives us the security we need to practice humility here on earth. As we do so, we remember that we are never forgotten—God always sees us because we are hidden in him.

Practical Application: Harnessing Humility

Have you ever been so embarrassed that you wished the floor would just open up and swallow you? Maybe you've known that feeling of humiliation so strong that you involuntarily squeezed your eyes shut, hoping against hope that it was all just a dream and you'd open your eyes to discover that nothing terrible had happened.

When we hear the word *humility*, it's easy to picture moments like these. Our brains naturally tie the word *humility* to *humiliation*. But the humility that Christ offers us is not about embarrassment or humiliation. It is about the radical peace, comfort, and freedom that come from embracing our position as one who is hidden with Christ in God.

We find a remarkable image of humility in Jesus himself, which the apostle Paul describes in Philippians 2:5–8.

In your relationships with one another, have the same mindset as Christ Jesus:

Who, being in very nature God,
did not consider equality with God something to be used
to his own advantage;
rather, he made himself nothing
by taking the very nature of a servant,

being made in human likeness.
And being found in appearance as a man,
he humbled himself
by becoming obedient to death—
even death on a cross! (NIV)

Based on the passage, write a definition of humility as exemplified by Jesus.

Jesus had every right to be lauded and honored during his earthly life. Instead, he chose a road so lowly that it did in fact lead to the very type of humiliation we spend so much of our lives trying to avoid. He endured the mocks, jeers, and violence of the crowd at his crucifixion out of love for us. He accepted death so that we might live. And in doing so, well, I'll let Scripture tell you:

Therefore God exalted him to the highest place
and gave him the name that is above every name,
that at the name of Jesus every knee should bow,
in heaven and on earth and under the earth,
and every tongue acknowledge that Jesus Christ is Lord,
to the glory of God the Father. (Phil. 2:9–11 NIV)

This passage shows us that Jesus's obedient humility led to his rightful occupation as Lord over all. This is our example of humility; this is our hope for heaven. No matter how low the road we walk in this life, the day of our exaltation is coming. We are hidden with Christ in God, awaiting the moment when he—and us with him—will be revealed.

How have you practiced humility in the past?

What would you like to see change about your habits of humility?

How might you pursue deeper humility in the coming days or weeks?

How might practicing humility as an expression of your hiddenness with Christ help you hope for heaven?

In closing, write a prayer describing the ways you want to practice humility in your daily life. Ask God to help you cultivate humility as one who is grateful to be hidden with Christ in God.

My Prayer for You

Dear God, you are so good to hide us in you. Thank you for ensuring our security in heaven. Help us to walk in humble gratitude for the ways you hold us now and will protect us forever. Amen.

HOLDING ON TO THE HOPE OF HEAVEN

Accompanies the Conclusion of The Hope of Heaven

I'm no longer fed up with this world. God has reminded me that there has always been a glorious plan in place. The scarlet thread of the grace and mercy of God began in the garden of Eden, crossed deserts and oceans and finally up to a hill called Calvary, then rose in triumph from the grave.

So now I'm looking up and I'm waiting and I'm expectant. We've not even begun to live. Hold on to Jesus. He is coming soon.

Sheila Walsh

Theme Scripture

Therefore, since we have been made right in God's sight by faith, we have peace with God because of what Jesus Christ our Lord has done for us. Because of our faith, Christ has brought us into this place of undeserved privilege where we now stand, and we confidently and joyfully look forward to sharing God's glory.

We can rejoice, too, when we run into problems and trials, for we know that they help us develop endurance. And endurance develops strength of character, and character strengthens our confident hope of salvation. And this hope will not lead to disappointment. For we know how dearly God loves us, because he has given us the Holy Spirit to fill our hearts with his love.

Romans 5:1–5

Reflection

What a journey this has been. I am so grateful that you have taken the time, energy, and effort required to think about and fix your eyes on heaven through this study. My prayer has been and will continue to be that fixing your eyes on heaven will fill you with the confidence and joy that the God who loves you is preparing a magnificent home for you.

In this concluding section, we're going to look at a word that we've seen many times throughout our study together: *hope*. We'll tie our word study and the practice of hope together.

I saved *hope* for the end because I want you to take this word with you as you go forward from here. May this final session together deepen, widen, and lengthen your hope for heaven.

Word Study: *Hope*

The final biblical term we're going to look at together is the Greek word *elpis* (ἐλπίς). I'll go ahead and tell you now—this word is translated as "hope" nearly always. As we look together at some passages containing *elpis*, let's turn our attention to the object of hope.

Underline what is hoped *for* in the following passages:

Her masters' hopes of wealth were now shattered, so they grabbed Paul and Silas and dragged them before the authorities at the marketplace. (Acts 16:19)

I asked you to come here today so we could get acquainted and so I could explain to you that I am bound with this chain because I believe that the hope of Israel—the Messiah—has already come. (Acts 28:20)

Isn't he really saying it for our sake? Yes, this is written for our sake, because he who plows ought to plow in hope, and he who threshes should thresh in hope of sharing the crop. (1 Cor. 9:10 CSB)

We are not boasting beyond measure about other people's labors. On the contrary, we have the hope that as your faith increases, our area of ministry will be greatly enlarged. (2 Cor. 10:15 CSB)

These passages help us see that while we typically think of hope in terms of our hope in Christ, the word itself, even in Scripture, simply refers to expectation or desire. What makes Christian hope so unique, good, and beautiful is what our hope is *in*—a secure Savior who will never fall short.

Take a look at a few more passages that specifically address our Christian hope.

I have the same hope in God as these men themselves have, that there will be a resurrection of both the righteous and the wicked. (Acts 24:15 NIV)

Such things were written in the Scriptures long ago to teach us. And the Scriptures give us hope and encouragement as we wait patiently for God's promises to be fulfilled. (Rom. 15:4)

But since we are of the day, let's be sober, having put on the breastplate of faith and love, and as a helmet, the hope of salvation. (1 Thess. 5:8 NASB)

Resurrection.
The fulfillment of God's promises.
Salvation.

These are the beautiful objects of our hope, the certainties that await us in eternity. In heaven, we will no longer have a need for hope, for everything we could ever long to see come to fruition will be our prize. We will see Jesus in all his glory, and our hope for our heavenly home will be satisfied once and for all.

 **Bridge**

It's time for us to take the truths we've learned all throughout this study and consider how we'll carry them with us in our thoughts and actions going forward. I hope you'll take the time to carve out a special moment for yourself—sit in a comfortable chair, pour a favorite beverage, or head to your go-to coffee shop—and join me in our final application section together.

Practical Application: Holding On to Hope

As we move on from here, let's equip ourselves with the tools we need to hold on to the hope of heaven. Whatever comes next in your life, may the word studies and practical applications you've learned here empower you to persevere with confidence and gladness in the future.

Take a moment to reflect on the truths we've learned about heaven:

- Heaven is a real place where we will live forever in a home prepared for us.
- When we die, we will immediately go to heaven to be with Jesus where there is fullness of joy.
- Everything we are hoping for will be there, and we will finally know true peace and joy.
- By placing our faith in Jesus, we are guaranteed a place in heaven.
- We know that when we get home, we will see and recognize our loved ones. All pain and shame will be gone, and we will join our voices with those of all our brothers and sisters through the ages and the millions of angels and worship Jesus as we've never done before.
- When we get home, every longing in our hearts will be fulfilled.
- One day, we will have the joy of standing before the judgment seat of Christ, our Savior and our Lord. When we place our trust in him, our salvation is eternally secure.
- We will live with Jesus forever in a new heaven and a new earth, where every day will be better than the one before. We will live and work and serve. We will be more alive than we have ever been.

- Our eternal identity is secure with Christ in heaven, and how we choose to live each day on earth now will add to the celebration in heaven when we are finally home.

With those truths in mind, consider which practical applications you want to focus on practicing in the coming months. Choose no more than three—getting overwhelmed is a recipe for giving up! Which of these applications will help you remember the truths that give you hope for heaven?

- Studying Scripture
- Journeying toward Joy
- Pursuing Peace
- Learning to Long
- Confessing to Connect
- Walking in Worship

- Persisting in Prayer
- Serving Faithfully
- Fostering Fellowship
- Harnessing Humility
- Holding On to Hope

On a separate piece of paper, for each practice you chose, write:

- *How* you will practice (e.g., "I will spend fifteen minutes each day intentionally cultivating joy.")
- *Whom* you will incorporate (e.g., "I will ask my friend to pray with me each week.")
- *When* you will practice (e.g., "I will serve at church once a month.")
- *What* will help you practice (e.g., "I will set an alarm on my phone to remind me to pray.")
- *Where* you will practice (e.g., "I will pursue peace by spending time in nature weekly.")
- *Why* you will practice (e.g., "I will practice fellowship through regular meals with others because deepening my relationships reminds me of the perfect community to come in eternity.")

Put the paper somewhere you'll see it regularly—maybe inside your Bible, on the refrigerator, or even framed on your desk. Check in with yourself every month or so to refresh, reset, and reenergize your effort to hold on to hope through spiritual practices.

Write a final prayer asking God to help you hold fast to the hope he has given you for a future with him.

_____

_____

_____

_____

My Prayer for You

Author of Hope, you are the One who will fulfill our every longing. Help us to cling to the truths we have learned about heaven so that we can remain faithful as we await our reunion with you. Thank you for preparing a place for us—we can hardly wait to see it. Amen.

Originally from Scotland, **Sheila Walsh** is an author, Bible teacher, and television host. She has spoken around the world to over six million people and now hosts numerous shows on TBN, America's most-watched faith and family channel, including the flagship show, *Praise*, and the talk show *Better Together*, reaching a potential daily audience of two billion people through TV and the TBN app.

A two-time Grammy-nominated recording artist, Sheila has recorded over twenty-five albums.

She loves making the Bible practical and sharing how God met her at her lowest point and helped her to rise up again.

Sheila's books have sold almost six million copies and include multiple bestsellers: *It's Okay Not to Be Okay*, *Praying Women*, and *Holding On When You Want to Let Go*.

She and her husband, Barry, live in Texas with their crazy little dog, Maggie. Their son, Christian, is a clinical psychologist.

Connect with Sheila:

SheilaWalsh.com

@SheilaWalshConnects

@SheilaWalsh1

@SheilaWalsh

Watch Sheila on the Trinity Broadcasting Network, America's largest faith and family network.